MW01274860

Amazon reviews of *Freedom from Luggage*'s first version:

"It is well written and concise in its details. My luggage is now smaller and easily accommodates my travel needs. ... A wonderful, practical little book."

"I'm a flight attendant (30 years) and loved the Andersen's take on how to pack light to simplify travel.... I plan to use their techniques on my next vacation!"

"Having seen this in practice and had the authors stay at our B and B in CHCH NZ. I can say the book is a fab. summary of how they travel. ... I will recommend the book to all guests as it really is the planet friendly way to travel as it uses less resources on so many different levels... just think of all the saved jet fuel!!!"

"Wonderful and well thought out. I will use many of these ideas. The pictures are very helpful and motivating."

"...I found your book extremely helpful. So many times I have returned from a trip and found myself unpacking many unworn items that I brought 'just in case.'"

"For someone like me (who tends to "travel heavy"), the book was a revelation, and I recommend it to anyone planning an overseas or domestic journey."

Freedom from Luggage

How to Pack Light for
European Travel
and Beyond

Roger and Kyanne Andersen

Freedom from Luggage

Table of Contents

Introduction

Imagine yourself as a tourist arriving at a new destination on a plane, bus, or train. While others wrestle with their luggage, you simply exit, ready to start your vacation. The travel clothes you're wearing go with carefully-chosen additional garments that add variety and flexibility. They join toiletries in a light shoulder bag or small daypack about the size and weight of a gallon of milk. That's it.

No wheeled suitcase. Luggage-free travel.

We've written this book so others could enjoy the liberation we've experienced on two-month long trips around New Zealand and Europe. We've also learned from numerous cruises around regions stretching from Thailand east to Turkey. Those trips and land forays elsewhere have kept us busy for about four months each year. We're not business travelers, just two retired folks who like to see new places and hate to lug stuff around. We've found it both liberating and surprisingly easy to take less.

We start by focusing on entirely eliminating the suitcase because most of us have never considered that option. Freedom from luggage particularly suits travel with numerous stops on public transportation, like taking trains around Europe or buses around New Zealand. The principles also work for anyone with limited storage space: bikers, cyclists, hikers.

Moreover, aiming to eliminate luggage prompts new thinking about all travel. Sometimes, you just need more stuff. Golf requires clubs. Some medical conditions require equipment. Advanced photography, multiple lenses. Sometimes you just want dressier clothes or more variety. As an example, we devote a chapter to packing for a cruise or bus tour. The lessons highlighted there apply to anyone - including those traveling with children - who needs luggage. With the basics efficiently covered, it's easier to handle the desired extras.

We invite you to explore ideas for more easily traveling our world.

Chapter 1

Escaping
from Luggage

We've learned that travel without luggage lifts the spirit by eliminating many burdens and adding a sense of adventure. Put aside for the moment concerns about how you'd do without the stuff you typically carry. We'll get there. Consider first a bakers' dozen advantages of escaping from luggage.

1 - Easier Carrying On

Most of us have struggled to fit a roll-around into an overhead airplane bin. Maybe ours is heavy, or fellow passengers have left little room, or both.

No luggage, no lifting.

2 - Keeping Your Stuff

How often have you wondered if your stuff will disappear along the way? Will you claim your checked luggage before someone else does? How about that carry-on stowed in the shared luggage section of a train car?

No luggage, no lost luggage.

3 - Saving Money

Travel without luggage saves more than baggage charges. You don't need a cab just to move the luggage. Or airport "red hats" and hotel bellhops to carry it. No fares. No tips.

No luggage, more money.

4 - Easier Ascent

Stairs are everywhere. They add variety to plazas and elegance to public buildings. They're almost as commonplace as street corners. We climb down to subways or up to a friend's home. Onto buses and trains and into countless stores and offices. They are so much a part of our daily lives that, unless our mobility is limited, we hardly notice them.

Until we travel and charming streets become barriers.

Or we need to reach a train platform, and there's no conveyor belt like the one in Leipzig.

And then there's Venice.

No luggage, easier steps.

5 - Keeping Hands Free

Remember the challenge of pulling a roll-around into a coffee shop? Or out, with a hot cup in one hand? Or through a small revolving door? Or while keeping track of a child?

Ever propped open the motel room door with one bag so you could try to pull another one through the limited space remaining? Or blocked open an elevator door so you could load all the suitcases or the luggage cart?

How about needing to grab a balance pole or strap on a crowded airport shuttle or subway?

No luggage, free hands.

6 - Efficient Trips

When traditional travelers get to a new place, lodging often becomes the first stop. Before they eat, shop, visit an attraction, or walk through the park, they need to drop off luggage. In contrast, traveling without luggage facilitates visiting spots along the way. Minimal stuff maximizes opportunities to do what you came to do.

Increased freedom works at the other end, too. When a morning check-out combines with a later-in-the-day departure, traditional travelers are stuck with stuff. Sometimes they can check it at the lodging, but then they have to swing back before moving on to the next stop. Each of those trips takes valuable time (and sometimes money).

No luggage, fewer trips.

7 - Saving Energy

Ours and the planet's. Luggage with wheels carry weight, but weight is still the enemy.

And sometimes so are the wheels.

Even crossing quaint cobblestone plazas gets old.

When we wear out just getting to and from our lodging, our vacation suffers.

Further, whatever we bring along when not walking or cycling also requires another kind of energy -- usually from fossil fuels -- to move us and our stuff. Savings from each of us add up to a cooler planet.

Less stuff, more energy.

8 - Less Anxiety

The more separate things we carry, the more difficulty we have when we stop along the way -- waiting at an airport gate, recharging in a coffee

shop. When it's time to leave, do we have everything? Purse? Jacket? Carry-on? Suitcase(s)?
Then there's the lodging. How much luggage
can the room handle? Can you settle in and relax?
On day 2, is there room to sit down? Which clothes
are clean? On the final morning, missing anything?

Fewer items, less anxiety.

9 - More Free Time

Limiting one freedom of choice -- what we'll
wear -- increases another -- what we'll do. Unpacking at a new place is a breeze. Fewer options
means less time (and strain) each morning deciding what to wear. Quicker repacking leaves more
time to sleep-in on travel days.

Less stuff, more time.

10 – Easier Laundering

For any trip longer than about a week, we end
up having to do laundry or bring more clothes. The
more clothes we add, the bigger the suitcase. And
that may not save the laundry stop anyway. The
traditional approach to laundry includes the hassle
of finding a place and taking the time to wash and
dry clothes. Taking fewer, lighter clothes eases the
burden.
Washing small items in the bathroom sink and
hanging them to air dry overnight takes only a few

minutes and frees daytime hours for more enjoyable activity. Even if you are staying in a place with laundry facilities, quick-dry clothes either shorten the time waiting for a dryer to finish or allow skipping that step by simply hanging up the clothes.

Lighter clothes, easier laundering.

11 – Expanded Opportunities

From Cinque Terra to Venice and Ptuj to Dubrovnik, European travel, in particular, offers innumerable chances to experience the culture up close in small hotels, traditional B&B's, and air B&B's.

However, these interesting places are often along cobblestone lanes.

Or up steep, multi-stair walkways.

Inside, more stairs lead higher to charming, sometimes small, rooms.

Eliminating luggage helps us embrace these opportunities and their challenges.

No luggage, easier options.

12 – Spontaneity

Once you have developed a separate wardrobe and set of toiletries for travel, you can be ready to leave in minutes. Escaping for a few days can be as easy as going out for pizza. You're always ready. On a trip you'd like to extend? No problem. You already have what you need.

Moreover, reserving a small set of clothes just for travel enhances the sense of change that makes vacations enjoyable. And getting them out again will bring back memories.

Travel clothes, easier escapes.

13 – Romance

Hold hands instead of luggage.

Chapter 2

Shifting to Travel Mode

Many of us start our vacation packing by counting the number of days we'll be gone and deciding whether or when we expect to do laundry. Then we pick out clothes and locate outerwear and bathroom necessities. The closer the packing is to our departure time, the greater the temptation to panic and add a few other items "just in case" we haven't thought of everything. Only then do we select whatever bag (or bags) we'll need to carry that much stuff.

We can free ourselves to better enjoy our vacations by shifting our thinking from "daily stuff moved someplace else" to "travel mode." By assembling a separate travel wardrobe with accessories ahead of time, we can eliminate or minimize the need for luggage.

For many women especially, reaching this goal may require adjustment. At home we often aim to create a "perfect ensemble" for each situation: the distinctive top, the right pants or skirt, the footwear with the perfect height and matching purse. But this approach requires a closet of clothes. To travel "light," we have to be more flexible.

Think of a travel wardrobe like uniform options you might have once had in school or at work. Only this time it's one you have chosen. One you know you look good in. One that fits your sense of style. One that you can vary for the occasion.

We pack multiple shirts or pants or skirts with two principal needs in mind: backup and variety. If we drip mustard at lunch -- or get caught in a downpour -- we want something else to wear to dinner. But we really only need one extra outfit to meet that concern. Many of us don't want to wear (or see a companion in) the same outfit every day. But careful choices and a few accessories can support several "looks" with the same clothes.

By investing in travel clothes, eliminating extras, and redefining "luggage," we can shift into travel mode. When we do need more than the bare minimum, we still benefit by getting more stuff into smaller space with less weight.

A. Selecting Travel Clothes

The first step in shifting to travel mode is developing a small, specialized wardrobe of clothes that will dry overnight. You may already have some things that fit the bill, but may want to invest in some light-weight, quick-dry, wrinkle-free clothes.

Products developed for backpackers, cyclists, and runners often work great. However, sports-oriented clothes may look too informal for some situations. In response, numerous suppliers include options with a dressier look and feel.

After identifying basic principles to keep in mind, this section describes how to build a wardrobe and then provides sample lists for women and men.

1. Basic Principles

To build the smallest, lightest, easiest to care for, and most flexible wardrobe possible —

Consider the Fabric
The more any fabric has the following characteristics, the better:
>light-weight
>quick-drying
>ability to stay wrinkle-free
>odor resistance built-in
>ability to hold shape after being wrung out
>durability
>snag resistance
>stain resistance
>ability to wick away perspiration
>UV protection, if appropriate

The first three elements are the most important.

First, lighter fabric both weighs less and takes up less space. For illustration, compare the stacks pictured below of (1) five short-sleeved cotton T-shirts for home wear, one pair of cotton pants, and one jersey knit skirt and (2) five travel T-shirts, one pair of travel pants, and a nylon travel skirt. Actually, our minimalist list below doesn't include this much, but whatever the numbers, lighter fabric matters.

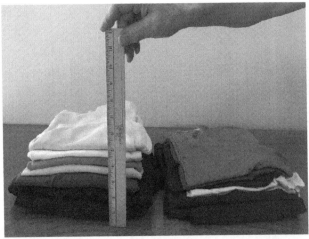

Second, the clothes need to dry overnight.

Third, after multiple wearings and washings, they shouldn't look like they've been slept in.

Synthetics and blends usually work best. You can learn a lot by crunching up a shirttail to judge both weight and wrinkle-resistance. Most cotton weighs too much, takes up too much space, wrinkles too easily, and takes too long to dry. However, if you really want jeans, one pair can work if you wear (instead of carry) them on travel days and have something else to wear while they dry.

Maximize Compatibility

To maximize the number of different looks available in the wardrobe, every item should be able to be worn with virtually every other item. Black or gray pants/skirts allow tops to introduce a variety of colors. Lighter neutrals such as khaki or beige can work, but get dirty more easily.

Check the Pockets

We all want to carry some items nearly all the time: wallet, comb, phone.... They need places, and adequate pockets provide them. Clothes designed for travel often include zippered and hidden pockets to protect valuables. Be sure they are large enough to hold what you plan to put there.

Use Layers

To handle a variety of situations and temperatures, think in terms of layers. For example, as needed, a shirt can layer over a basic tee/tank, topped in turn with a sweater/vest and a rainproof shell jacket.

Double-dip

Plan for alternative uses. A t-shirt can be sleepwear. At least for men, a swimsuit doubles for treks

17

to a restroom down the hall (and something to wear while washing pants).

Watch the Weight
Just as with our bodies, the wardrobe's total weight can creep up on you.

2. Steps for Building a Travel Wardrobe

An efficient, varied wardrobe starts with basic elements and carefully adds interesting options.

Window Shop
One good place to start is by wandering a sporting-goods store that carries a number of brands. Compare different combinations. Do you like pull-overs or button-fronts? Does an over-shirt work better than a sweater? Which works best alone? Or over something else? Are multi-pocketed pants too casual?

When you find a brand you like, it helps to find a store or website featuring that brand. They'll likely offer more selection. However, beware of online shopping unless you've actually felt the fabric. "Lightweight" and "wrinkle-resistant" have variable meanings.

Remember the Little Stuff (and Skip the Purse?)
While examining individual clothing options, imagine where smaller items will go and how they will

fit. Women may want to reconsider the habit of carrying a purse. If items once carried in a purse can fit in pockets, there's one fewer thing to carry, keep track of, and move out of the way. Crucial items can go in pants or skirt pockets to keep them with you.

It's helpful to bring along whatever you think you'll carry in shirt and pants pockets. Try them out. How comfortable is the "loaded" clothing? How easily could a pickpocket remove the items? How hard are they to get out when you want them?

Start near the Bottom
Pants or skirts -- the items worn most often -- form the base of a wardrobe. They're also among the heaviest and bulkiest, so they make a good place to start building.

A durable, lightweight synthetic pant is probably your best bet. For warmth, consider adding long underwear instead of selecting heavier fabric. That way, one pair of pants may be enough. Principal attributes will be having plenty of pockets and a color compatible with multiple tops. By having a few pockets and carefully selecting what she needs to keep with her, Kyanne has been able eliminate carrying a purse. She loves the freedom.

Convertible pants add an opportunity to combine efficiency with flexibility. The lower legs zip off to create shorts, and zip back on when temperatures cool.

Convertibles, however, have a less-dressy look. All need the zipper above the knee. Some are cargo pants, with large patch pockets. Because they do not fit as tightly, outside pockets pose a greater security risk. Roger once lost a wallet from a zippered patch pocket. He's since shifted to casual slacks with zippered pockets. He now carries the convertibles for the shorts.

Jeans, so useful and comfortable at home, present two problems as travel wear. Their weight and bulk leave them ill-suited for packing. That's OK, so long as you can wear them on travel days. They also don't air-dry overnight. You need something else to wear either at the laundromat or on the drying day.

Women may want to consider selecting (or adding) a lightweight skirt or shift dress to provide both a dressier look and a substitute for shorts. Kyanne loved having a simple black dress in Europe, instead of the shorts she took to New Zealand. It served just as well as shorts for walking the beaches on hot days (worn with bare legs) and easily dressed up in the evening with tights and scarves or jewelry. European women tend to wear dresses, so she fit right in.

If you don't carry a purse, any skirt or dress will likely need pockets. Skirts and dresses with invisible zipper pockets are now available.

Coordinate Tops

Coordinating choices is both the most time-consuming and the most valuable wardrobe-building task. Re-combining just a few pieces can create many different "looks."

For example, consider five items, chosen so the colors can go together: a short-sleeve knit t-shirt; a long-sleeve knit t-shirt; a long-sleeve, button-front, woven shirt; a neutral colored skirt, and a pair of neutral-colored slacks that coordinate with any of the tops. They can combine to create different "looks".

Each t-shirt can be worn alone. The woven shirt can be

worn buttoned up. Either t-shirt can be worn under the woven shirt that is then left unbuttoned as an over-shirt. Any of the tops can be worn with the skirt instead of the pants.

Just five items provide variety while covering different temperatures and levels of formality. Add a lightweight scarf, a belt, or a necklace and the options multiply.

Those particular looks may not suit your style. Simply apply the general principle: every item should be able to be worn with virtually every other item. For example, you may prefer to layer with a lightweight cardigan instead of the woven shirt, or have a reversible vest to add variety. Perhaps you prefer silky shells or tank tops instead of traditional t-shirts. Coordinate a few lightweight, packable items that can be dressed up or down and layered for warmth. Make it your own.

Rethink underwear and socks

Cotton underwear and many padded bras have trouble drying overnight. Look for underwear styles that are comfortable, quick-drying, odor-resistant, and durable enough to handle daily washing.

Lightweight silk, wool, or synthetic long underwear tops and bottoms offer warmth for considerably less bulk and weight than a heavy jacket or heavier pants.

Socks can be more of a challenge. If too thin, they don't provide enough cushion for a day of walking. If too thick, they have trouble drying, especially if they are mostly cotton. We've settled on Merino wool socks. We carry a spare pair in case one gets (or stays) wet. Like the other clothing, it's best to feel the fabric before selecting the product.

Consider shoes

Comfortable walking shoes may be enough. If so, you'd have the distinct advantage of wearing, instead of carrying, what you need. Be sure they're broken-in. Before deciding to bring an extra pair, consider how often you'd really want to wear them, weighing that (literally) against the regular hassle of carrying them.

Everybody's feet differ. Kyanne raves about her black leather flats with enough built-in arch support  to eliminate her need for orthotics. They allow her to walk comfortably all day and still are acceptable with either slacks or a dress.

Roger has struggled to find a single shoe that meets all his wishes. Leather sneakers worked well in New Zealand when he wore very casual convertible pants anyway. Once he shifted to casual slacks, he would have liked shoes a bit more dressy when Kyanne was dressing up. Sneaker failure prompted an emergency purchase of black oxfords. They look clunky with shorts. Unless cold weather is contemplated, he's trying sandals that can accommodate socks.

Women may opt to carry collapsible sandals that can go with a skirt for a dressier option. They don't offer as much support, but may work well for short periods and are light to carry.

Boots are a little like jeans. If they are chosen as the main staple footwear, they must go with everything, be worn on travel days, and be extremely comfortable to walk in.

Avoid bulky knits

A simple cardigan sweater can take the chill off of cooler days or evenings. It can also serve as a swimsuit coverup in a pinch. However, some sweaters can both add weight and take up lots of space. In contrast, Merino wool deserves its reputation for being light and warm.

Invest in outerwear

A lightweight, waterproof jacket, perhaps with a hood, may be the best outerwear choice. It should be able to collapse to a small space, yet provide protection and warmth when layered with other clothes. A packable hat can provide warmth as well as  rain and sun protection.

Fit Right In

A travel wardrobe sensitive to a range of cultural norms will work in more places. Jeans and sandals, as common as they are, may be disrespectful in some settings. Women especially should consider the advantages of modesty. In many places, our hosts would view low-cut, tight tops and short shorts as inappropriate dress. Carry a scarf for an emergency head covering or swimsuit cover-up. European women wear skirts more often than women do in the U.S. European men seldom wear shorts. Fitting-in is both safer and more respectful.

Like your choices

When you travel, you'll be wearing these clothes a lot. Be sure you like them. You really only need a handful of basic coordinating items. Except for travel companions who will either be sharing your approach or wishing they had, you won't see the same people every day. You can look sharp in the same clothes you wore the day before – and no one has to know.

3. What to Wear, What to Carry

The prior sections' principles fit together to allow you to create a small, light, easy to care for, basic wardrobe. Because layering can accommodate a wide temperature range, our basic clothing lists work well for a temperate climate. Each day, you can achieve whatever number of layers you need by selecting among a jacket, a sweater, a long-sleeve shirt, and a t-shirt.

Rather than waiting until the night before leaving, wardrobe selection should accompany itinerary planning. Expected weather may call for some adjustments to your basics list.

For cooler climes, even a light scarf breaks the wind. Consider quick-drying long underwear. Look for a hat that can both provide warmth and protect from rain and sun. Lightweight knit gloves can live in jacket pockets, but make a big difference if it's cold.

If you expect heat, add shorts or a skirt. Before adding swimwear, consider the likelihood of actually using it. Recall that you aren't going to the end of the world. If the weather surprises, invest in a souvenir.

Moving between regions with large temperature differences may require luggage to handle the additional clothes. On the other hand, you may be able to send things ahead to await your arrival. Or carry a coat for a while and then mail it home. We bought sweaters as New Zealand souvenirs and mailed them home after leaving the mountains.

The particular lists below might not fit your personal situation. Different trips (and different travelers) have different requirements. However, as you consider our suggestions keep two points in mind: (1) having once found something handy does not justify carrying it on every trip and (2) the longer your list, the more you ultimately have to move to the next stop.

Intended for modification in light of climate, destination, and personal preferences, here are our suggestions for the basics. You might cut the list further by eliminating some of the "2nd" options. On the other hand, we've learned that adding a second coordinated overshirt or skirt multiples the combinations available. We're happier having more choices while still avoiding luggage.

Women's Clothing Checklist

Worn on travel days:
Jacket and sweater, as needed
Long-sleeved over-shirt/blouse
T-shirt
Pants Underwear
Bra
Socks
Shoes
Hat (or hood on jacket)

Carried:
Jacket and sweater, unless worn
2nd long sleeved overshirt/blouse
2nd T-shirt

Shorts, short skirt, or extremely lightweight
    dress
2nd underwear
2nd bra
2nd pair socks
Light scarf
Nightwear, if desired

Men's Clothing Checklist

Worn on travel days:
Jacket and sweater, as needed
Long-sleeved buttoned shirt
T-shirt
Pants
Belt (moneybelt?)
Undershorts
Socks
Shoes
Hat (or hood on jacket)

Carried:
Jacket and sweater, unless worn
T-shirt
2nd pair socks
2nd underwear
Shorts (or convertibles)

The Result: A Couple's Closet

B. Eliminating Extras

We now turn our attention to ways to limit those extras that seem to multiply -- like hangers in a closet -- in our travel collections. Then we highlight our favorite essentials.

Sharing
We can save weight and space by applying a lesson from kindergarten. Sharing is good: sun block, insect repellant, over-the-counter meds, toothpaste, nail clippers, comb .... Partners may be able to use the same unscented (?) deodorant and share a razor handle. We have found that both

men's and women's blades can fit on the same handle.

Multiple Uses

Double-dipping helps again. Lodging-supplied bar soap, or even shower gel, may also work for shaving cream. Shampoo doubles for hand laundry.

Smart phones or small tablets with can hold a carry-on's worth of items: address list, alarm clock, boarding passes, camera, flashlight, games, guidebooks, itinerary, calculator, notepaper, maps, pens, recreational books, reservation confirmations.

Medications

Prescription medications require planning ahead to avoid running out; insurance companies often give vacation waivers that allow you to collect a large enough supply. Individual types of meds usually fit in small plastic bags that save space by flattening over time. Label them to avoid confusion. A one-week sorter works well (in a bag for safety); re-sort as you would at home. Bring written prescriptions if you'll need refills.

International travel may require labeled prescription bottles. A local pharmacy may be able to use small bottles that won't waste as much space as the mail order containers. Ours provides separate labels we attach to small plastic bags (purchased at a bead store) instead.

A few headache, stomach, and intestinal pills may come in handy, but not whole bottles. Unless you are leaving civilization, refills will be available. Colds usually give some advance notice, allowing time to get medicine on the road. A couple of Band-Aids don't take much space, but the first-aid kit can (usually) stay at home with the rest of the medicine cabinet.

If you are traveling internationally and use particular non-prescription remedies daily (e.g., antacids or allergy meds), treat them like prescription drugs: bring enough for the whole trip. At least in Italy and Austria, any medicine you ingest must be bought in a pharmacy. They have limited hours and don't display those items on open shelves. Communicating your needs to someone behind the counter can be a challenge, especially in a foreign language with unfamiliar brands. Be aware that some countries restrict or prohibit drugs that are legal to carry in the U.S.

Keys & Wallets
Keys not needed on the trip are safer at home; we leave all of them and rely upon our garage door opener code when we return. Same rule for most of those cards in the wallet; we each carry a driver's license, emergency info, an all-purpose credit card with a different number from the one the other person is carrying (as a backup in case one is lost), and a cash card.

Makeup & Accessories
Women may be able to replace an entire makeup drawer with tinted moisturizer, a small

mascara tube, and a lipstick. Mini-compacts combine blush, bronzer and eye shadow.

A simple, light chain necklace can stand alone or carry a variety of dangles. Starting with a few earrings works well; new ones make great souvenirs while taking up little space.

A lightweight scarf or two can add wardrobe variety while also providing a head cover for religious sites.

A new haircut or more frequent hair washing may eliminate the desire for a curling iron. Round brushes and a hair dryer work for some people instead of a curling iron. Most accommodations provide hair dryers.

Securing Valuables

Security devices come in all sorts of designs. Some fit down in a pair of pants, secured by a loop over the belt. Others hang from the neck or strap around the waist under a shirt. Those with breathable fabric are more comfortable against the skin in hot weather. Some designs come with special liners to prevent scanners from identifying credit cards or passports stored inside. Belts with inside zippers can look normal while holding emergency cash.

Assess the security risks of a particular trip before deciding what style to take. What's inconvenient for a thief is also inconvenient for you.

Similarly, consider the risks at different stages of travel when choosing what to put inside the security device. As a general rule, carefully stash passport, credit cards and most cash. To avoid having to undress before paying for a cup of coffee, consider keeping some cash easily available. Some airport security checks require removing all paper from your person, so plan ahead. Rick Steves suggests using a carabiner to attach bags to the upper rack in a train. That discourages others from grabbing something on the way by, especially in a dark tunnel.

Non-clothing Checklist
Here's a start at developing your own "essentials" list. If you are tempted to add something that's not listed here, however, ask if you really need it.

Electronics
Phone/tablet
Charging plugs and cords - some have multiple
    USB outlets
Back up battery(ies) for recharging on the go

Toiletries
Meds (prescription and minimal over-the-coun
    ter)
Toothbrush/floss
Toothpaste
Razor & blades
Deodorant
Shampoo (small, as backup)
Comb
Sun block, if needed
Insect repellent, if needed
Moisturizer/makeup, if desired

Feminine hygiene supplies
Birth control, if desired
3 Band-Aids/ Polysporin

Miscellaneous
Nail clippers/tweezers/emery board
Jewelry
Travel curling iron, if desired
Clothesline(s)
Sunglasses
Driver's License (picture ID)
Emergency contact info
Medication alerts and list
Credit/debit/ATM cards
Card numbers & phone numbers (stored sepa
    rately)
Place(s) to hold change/currency
Secure pouch / money-belt
Clear quart bag for liquids
Earplugs / sleep mask for a light sleeper

International Travel
Passport
Adapter plug(s)
Pen for filling out forms
Proof of sufficient solvency
Prescriptions or doctor's letter
Travel visa, if necessary

Personal Favorite Convenience Products
    Just like any products we mention, we don't re-
ceive any incentive or compensation from any of
these companies.

Sea to Summit nylon sling bag or daypack. Handy when you need it and out of the way when you don't. [That's a dime.]

Sea to Summit Aeros Pillow Ultralight (Amazon $40) that stuffs into a sack only slightly larger than the one pictured above. Kyanne likes a deeper pillow than many European hotels offer, and by placing this slightly-inflated pillow underneath, she adjusts the height of hotel pillows. It's also useful on the plane, on trains when the seats are too deep, and on the ferry for a nap on a bench.

Nite Ize's S-Binder with MicroLock hooks together dual zippers. It's not strong enough to stop someone from breaking into a stored bag, but it would stop almost anyone from unzipping a bag while you were carrying it. [That's a quarter.]

Violife Slim sonic toothbrush. Compact and self-contained- 1.6 oz, ($23). [That's a quarter.]

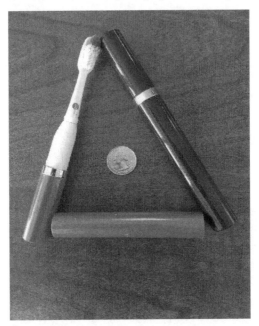

Travelon Net Packing Squares from Eddie Bauer. Smallest for seldom used, middle size for electronic plugs/cords and batteries, large for daily use. ($20 set of three)

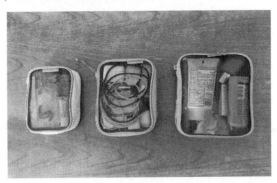

Freedom i-Connex folding keyboard. Especially while riding trains, we draft travel notes and insert photos into a Pages file. The keyboard allows us to work quietly instead of using the voice recognition feature that could disturb other passengers. It works with any Bluetooth-equipped device.

Chapter 3

Rethinking "Luggage"

You know by now that we encourage you to consider whether you really need a roll-around carry-on. With hands free of luggage, life opens up. We can both open doors and carry an ice cream cone. We can hold both hands and handrails. But we still have to carry some stuff. Fortunately, there are good alternatives to wheeled luggage.

A. Carrying Lightly

As you learn about our choices and search for something appropriate for yourself, understand that we are short people, with small clothes. You may simply need a bit more space than we do. However, recall a familiar problem with life in general. Size and weight can creep up on us unnoticed. Even if you're skipping a suitcase, you may find yourself considering a fancy backpacker's getup with more space than you need and weight than you want.

Also, think twice about products that incorporate wheels into backpacks. They offer the superficial attraction of being able to switch between the modes. But the wheel mechanisms add significant weight that will always be there. (REI's "Travel Pack" is 8 lbs. 14 oz; Rick Steves' "Rolling Backpack" is 5 1/2 lbs.) Moreover, shifting to using them on "level" ground forfeits the hands-free advantages we identified at the start.

After some trial and error, we've each identified an option that fits our individual needs and preferences. (We'll save the history for an Appendix, in case you're interested.) Kyanne prefers something slung over one shoulder, so it can be moved easily from one side to the other or held in front. Roger would rather wear something on his back, getting a balanced load despite the increased security risk and the relative difficulty of putting it on.

Now that we are getting specific about brand name products, we should explain that we don't receive any incentive or compensation from any of these companies. We just want to offer the most helpful information we can.

We've each found a Rick Steves product that we like. Although both are marketed as day bags, we use them for basic travel. Kyanne has selected the Civita Shoulder Bag (pictured left, next page). Made of microfiber, it comes with an adjustable padded strap and weighs 10 oz. There's an 11x9x3 main pocket, an 8x9x1 1/2 front pocket, and a third, thinner front pocket for flat items. Each side carries a spot appropriate for a water bottle, or an extra pair of socks, or a nylon stuff sack for groceries.

Roger favors the Civita Daypack (pictured above, right). Made of microfiber with padded straps, it weighs 10 oz. The overall dimensions of 14x11x5 1/2 include the same mix of pockets as the Civita shoulder bag, except the large, flat one on the back. Each is available on-line from Rick Steves and in 2019 cost $25. [Caution: the other Rick Steves daypack, Ravenna, is larger and considerably heavier.]

To cover the day trip needs the Rick Steves bags are marketed for, we instead each bring a Sea to Summit nylon sling bag or backpack like the one shown here. Weighing 2.2 oz, they easily hold lunch and jacket or sweater for a walk or short hike and are handy as a shopping bag. If needed, they can also serve as a way to move larger souvenirs accumulated over several days or locations until a trip to the post office is warranted. When not in use they pack in their own attached pouches.

B. Packing Techniques

The small outside pockets in our bags work great for stowing stuff like toiletries, electronics, the extra nylon bag, a water bottle, and even socks. We collect smaller items in structured and zippered mesh containers or quart plastic bags divided by category: daily use (e.g.,toothpaste), seldom used (e.g.fingernail clippers), and electronics.

To maximize space in the large pocket, we either tightly roll clothes or place them in plastic bags with the air squeezed out. Compared to simply folding clothes, both techniques conserve space, ease organization, and reduce wrinkling.

Rolling works better for knits than for woven shirts that may, despite careful selections, wrinkle more easily. You might find helpful a few YouTube "rolling travel clothes" videos. One caution: they may encourage you to pack more than you need. Even when clothes take up less space, they add weight.

Roger likes a technique that uses the shirt's bottom edge to create a pouch.

Kyanne believes creating the pouch causes more wrinkles, so she skips that step. She usually wears the tops untucked, so wrinkles along the bottom can be prominent. Except towards the end of a cruise, Roger usually hides any wrinkles by tucking in.

Woven travel shirts tend to be slippery, so unroll easily. Creating the pocket can be a challenge, but it provides more stability than just rolling.

Kyanne prefers to fold any woven, buttoned shirt and slide it into a gallon-sized Ziplock <u>freezer</u>

bag to reduce wrinkling. (The "storage bag" version is not durable enough to last the trip. Larger compression bags are available for items that won't fit into a freezer bag.) Once compressed to remove air, the bag fits flat along the back of her shoulder bag's large compartment. (Roger thinks his similar shirts look just fine even after rolling.)

Unless rain or wind is too much, we stow the jackets and use the more accessible sweaters for warmth. The same "bag and com-

press" method works for the nylon shell jacket.

C. How It All Works: An Example from Europe

Minimalist packing lists and general suggestions offer a start at developing a travel wardrobe, but it can be hard to see how they can be applied to particular situations. To offer something more concrete, here we describe the adjustments we made for a 2018 trip to Europe.

Knowing when we travelled, what we expected to do, and where we went should help you place our packing decisions in context. To avoid summer crowds and prices, we toured on our own from May 1 to June 20. To narrow our temperature range, we moved mostly from south to north as summer arrived. (As it turned out, over a 10 day period in June we hit our warmest daily high of about 80 degrees Fahrenheit in Padua, Italy, and our coolest daily high of about 40 in Gornergrat, Switzerland.)

We've seen enough large cities for a while, so prefer smaller places that mix access to informal eateries with walks in hills or along beaches. We aim for a pace that gives us 3 nights at each stop, with a 4-5 night break near the middle. We're not serious hikers, but do follow easier trails into the mountains or to neighboring towns. We need neither dressy clothes nor hiking boots.

After a short stay in London/Cambridge, we flew to Zagreb, Croatia, and used planes, ferries, and busses to work as far south as Dubrovnik and back. Then trains carried us in an uneven arc through Slovenia and western Austria into northern Italy, ending in the Swiss Alps.

With those expectations in mind, we took the following clothes, wearing or carrying them as appropriate. We identify brand names to provide the most complete picture possible. We don't receive any incentive or compensation from any of these companies.

Kyanne's Europe Wardrobe

Black Eddie Bauer Travex pants with zipper pockets; 2 Brooks Runhappy short-sleeve T-shirts; one REI short-sleeve T-shirt; 2 long-sleeve button-front blouses; one short, black skirt; silk scarf; 2 pair black Fox River crew socks; one bra; two pairs Jockey underwear; one pair black tights; one black Citizen cashmere zip front sweater; one pair black Naot flats; black Eddie Bauer nylon shell jacket with hood; black thin knit gloves.

Roger's Europe Wardrobe

Beige Clothing Arts travel pants; beige Columbia convertible pants; black leather zippered moneybelt with emergency US cash; one ExOfficio short-sleeve T-shirt; one Brooks short-sleeve T-shirt; one UnderArmor coldgear long-sleeve T-shirt; one ExOfficio long-sleeve, button-down shirt; handkerchief; 2 pair Fox River beige crew socks; 1 pair black low-rise socks; beige Skechers shoes; 2 pair ExOfficio undershorts; one pair Merino wool long underwear bottoms; one black Citizen zip-front cashmere sweater; black Eddie Bauer Weatheredge jacket with hood removed; Tilley hat;

black thin knit gloves (lined leather gloves planned for purchase in Italy).

With all these garments and toiletries either worn or carried, our travel bags each weighed an easy-to-carry 6 pounds. Lighter than many women's purses!

_____

Now that you're packed and ready to go, let's take a further look at life on the road.

Chapter 4

Moving Along
without Luggage

As we've noted from the start, travel without luggage offers many advantages, mostly different aspects of convenience, over standard travel. Here we discuss a few issues that arise while on the road: laundry, souvenirs, and getting past official authorities.

A. Keeping Everything Clean

Taking a tightly-limited number of clothes necessarily means doing laundry more often, usually daily. But it's surprisingly easy to wash laundry in the sink before bed. We've found the evening hassle offset by the overall ease of getting from place to place. Moreover, daily laundry avoids the eventual need to locate, get to, wait at, and return from a laundry room or laundromat.

It takes about 10 minutes. On most nights we only need to wash the items that are the most vulnerable to absorbing odor -- the inner shirt, underwear, and socks. To keep the fabric clean over time, we wash those even if they're not smelly. Depending upon the weather and frequency of use, pants and over-shirts last considerably longer between washings. To stay on top of it without making laundry a big job, we'll sometimes add an over shirt to the mix one night and a pair of pants the next. If we find ourselves at a place with laundry facilities, we sometimes wash (almost) everything by machine for good measure.

A good hand-washing technique starts by filling the sink, using cold water if treating stains. If there's no stopper, a washcloth or even wadded tissue can substitute. Wet the fabric and apply soap directly to armpits, crotches, and spots. Any soap will do — dish soap, shampoo, even bar soap. Fortunately, lodgings are moving from bar soap to a hanging container of multi-purpose liquid soap, handy for laundry. Rub the treated areas against themselves enough to work up some lather and get it into the fabric. Then swish the laundry to wash the less-critical areas. Drain and squeeze out soapy water. Rinse <u>well</u> to avoid soap (and odor) buildup.

After the wringing out as much water as possible, spread the clothes on top of a towel on the floor, roll it into a tube, and walk on the tube. The goal is to get the clothes at least dry enough that they will not drip, so they can hang anywhere. (The towel should dry in time for a morning shower.)

The smaller and lighter the clothesline, the better. Two twisted elastic strands work much better

than a single solid line. That way, you can skip clothespins. Tucking undershorts into the line from the single-layer back side helps them dry more quickly.

Socks with fuzzy insides dry better inside out, hung from the top.

Hangers work especially well for shirts. Sometimes closets with open doors are fine, but look for good circulation: shower curtain rods, a secure lamp, a chair back ....

Finally, keep in mind that no one enjoys doing laundry -- especially someone else's underwear. Travel with a partner will go better if each person does their own hand washing and they share machine laundry duty.

B. Memories

Travelers without traditional luggage have fewer places to squirrel souvenirs. An extra collapsible bag like the one described in the "luggage" section works well. Of course, filling it will also mean carrying and keeping track of it. In any case, it helps to think small (earrings, bookmarks, key chains).

Otherwise, remember the mail. Many shops will handle all the details. Post offices often sell packaging. Instead of weighing down your travel, reminders of good times can meet you at home.

C. The Authorities

Skipping luggage doesn't really raise any new issues with security, customs, and immigration folks. We mention it because many people ask if they pose a problem.

Airport security officers are only concerned about what passengers are carrying. It's easy to simply run a jacket or light bag through the x-ray machine. Two things to remember: (1) liquids still need to be in a clear quart bag, and (2) you may have more pockets to empty.

We've never heard of a customs or immigration requirement to carry luggage. Be sure to have proper documentation and proof of financial resources.

Ironically, the only questions we've gotten have come at Air New Zealand check-ins. Suspicious clerks wondered why we had come so far without luggage. That gave us chances to explain the wonders of light travel.

We now turn to the mode of popular travel most associated with lots of luggage -- the cruise. Lessons from there apply to other common situations, where you may decide the benefits of carrying more outweigh the disadvantages, like on a bus tour.

Chapter 5

Packing for a Cruise / Tour

Many of us enjoy cruises. Lots of locales, yet unpacking only once. Meals in different settings, all within an easy walk. Convenient recreation and entertainment. Quiet spots to read. Travel days without planes, trains, or buses. A way to combine relaxation and exploration. Bus tours attract folks who enjoy land travel but lack the time or inclination to create their own schedules.

However, our attraction to luggage-free travel conflicts with classic images of a cruise terminal's rows of large suitcases facing delivery to various cabins. Or the smaller line awaiting a bus driver's stowing sometimes-smaller items into the luggage compartment. Or the airport lines at each end.

Most cruises call for dressier clothes at dinner. Some may call for hiking boots or diving gear. Bus tours that put smaller groups of people together over time may prompt a desire to carry more different clothes. Moreover, the combination of frequent moves, late nights, and early mornings may make daily laundry seem too much. All of that may require luggage, but we achieve a middle ground between "luggage-free" and "packed for a typical cruise/tour." This chapter explains how, but first we address why.

A. Finding a Middle Ground

Traditional cruise packing starts with casual "weekend wear" and a few nicer outfits appropriate for a dinner out. Many cruise lines move it up a notch at least some evenings, when tuxes and gowns may reign alone or mingle with suit coats and cocktail dresses. Then there's the sweatsuit and running shoes for the treadmill. And the swimsuit and cover-up to get to the hot tub or sun deck. Perhaps additional shore clothes and shoes would come in handy.

Bus tours don't require tuxes and exercise/swim options may not be on the agenda, but they may encourage more clothes simply because the relatively small group will be seeing each other every day. Variety may be a more important value than when you're on your own.

After all, what's the harm in a big suitcase or two? Many airports check bags at the curb. Baggage fees and tips are just part of travel cost. The destination airport may hire folks to help get stuff from baggage claim to a taxi. Or the cruise line may transfer luggage directly. In any case, once at the cruise terminal, luggage is the cruise line's problem.

Until it gets to the cabin or hotel room.

Most of us can't afford roomy cruise suites. Thus, a challenge: fitting all that stuff into a few drawers and small closets with a few hangers. Maybe more clothes can be folded and fit into the drawers. As long as they don't get too jammed in. Maybe the packing list included extra hangers. Will they fit on the rod? Will it matter if the shoes pile on top of each other? Maybe some items, planned for use later in the trip, can go under the bed in the suitcase. If it fits. Until they're needed. Then, "Where did I put that?!"

Experienced cruise passengers will recognize the parody in our description, but it illustrates a point. Even when other folks do most of the work, extra-large or extra-full suitcases can be a pain. Finally, early departure at the end of a cruise is a snap when you don't have much luggage.

On a smaller scale, bus tours pose similar issues. Nearly-daily moves preclude extensive unpacking, but place a premium on items being easier to find and laundry taking less time.

And there's still that problem of getting to, around, and from the airport.

So it's worth thinking about taking less.

B. Same Theory, New Setting

Now-familiar ideas allow us to both shrink and lighten what we carry on a cruise. Coordinated outfits reduce the need for more items. Quick-dry clothes are especially important for saving space and weight.

The lists below are for a one-week cruise with two "formal" dinners expecting women in fancier clothes and men in jackets and ties. (Cruises we've taken don't require gowns & tuxes. Some lines rent formalwear.) Near-daily laundry would handle underwear and socks; machine laundry would come mid-week. Items identified as "dress" are standard weight. Others are quick-dry.

Each of these lists fits into a roll-around carry-on small enough to fit under an airplane seat. Extras and accessories go in a collapsible nylon bag. With some tweaking, the lists can work for a bus tour or a business trip that also allows some time to relax.

1. A Woman's Cruise Clothing List

Casual:
4-5 short sleeved t-shirts, shells, or tanks. 2 long-sleeved button-front wrinkle-free blouses (or lightweight cardigans) that coordinate with t-shirts.
2 pair of slacks
walking shoes

Semi-casual (For non-formal-night dinners as desired):
1-2 long/short skirts which can be worn with tops above
scarves/jewelry to accessorize
dressy sandals (can double for formal wear shoes)

"Formal":
1a) soft black cocktail dress
   or
1((b) black silky slacks, palazzo pants, or long skirt and silky blouse

and

(2) a look-changer for the second formal night to go with the above (e.g., alternative blouse, shawl, lacy sweater, dressy jacket and coordinated dressy jewelry)

Sports:
    swimsuit
    gauze cover-up or wrap
    flip-flops   or   sandals   (may   also
    serve   for   "dressy   sandals"   mentioned
    above)
    exercise pant/top/shoes

Undergarments:
    2 pair underwear
    2 bras
    3 pair socks
    lightweight nightwear (optional)

Outerwear:
    light jacket (hood optional)
    hat (optional for sun & rain)

For cool weather add:
    lightweight wool sweater
    gloves

For warm weather add:
    lightweight crushable sundress
    shorts
    consider tank top(s) in place of
        1-2 t-shirts above

2. A Man's Cruise Clothing List

Casual:
Pants
3 t-shirts (long or short sleeved); double as
    undershirts under button-front shirts
1 polo shirt (for standard dinners)
2 button-front long-sleeved shirts
    (for standard dinners)
walking shoes

"Formal":
dress sport coat or suit coat
dress shirt
[below also for casual use]
dress slacks
dress socks
dress shoes

Sports:
swimsuit
running shorts/top/shoes
flip-flops

Undergarments:
2 pr. undershorts
2 pr. socks
lightweight nightwear (optional)

Accessories:
tie
belt

Outerwear:
light jacket (hood optional)
hat (for sun & rain)

For cool weather add:
lightweight wool sweater
wool cap (optional)
gloves (optional)

For warm weather add:
shorts (unless taking convertible pants)

C. Packing Techniques

The packing methods described in Chapter 2 apply to virtually all travel. Knits -- from t-shirts to formal wear -- can be rolled. Blouses and dress-shirts can be folded and placed in freezer bags with the air squeezed out. Scarves stay neat in a flat plastic bag. Dress slacks and jackets fold.

With the advantage of being relatively small, each of us takes a roll-around small enough to fit under most airplane seats (about 15"H x 15"W x 8"D). Extras and accessories sometimes go in a nylon shoulder bag.

Combining items from a luggage-free wardrobe with traditional dress-up clothes yields an easily manageable cruise carry-on. Here are two examples from a cruise.

Roger took these clothes:

The bottom layer of his suitcase had sock-filled shoes on each side and rolled items in the middle. Another layer of rolled items was topped by a dress shirt in a freezer bag, with dress pants folded just below a sportcoat.

Here's Kyanne's selection:

A combination of using freezer bags and stacking rolled items used the space efficiently. Medications and her share of extras fit in the outside front pockets.

Jacket on her arm, she's off to a cruise.

D. "Cruise Plus" Opportunities

To take better advantage of having spent air fare, travelers often combine cruises with other vacation stays. In addition to reviewing your packing list to be sure it accommodates the land portion, consider adding a packable shoulder bag or pack. You may be able to store your cruise suitcase temporarily and enjoy the rest of your trip without luggage.

For example, we took that approach to extend a Mediterranean cruise with a side trip to Hydra, Greece. First thing, we dropped our carry-ons at the Athens airport hotel for pickup later. Then a ferry ride and the freedom to climb hills and stairs before returning to Athens to collect the bags for our flight home.

Chapter 6

Deciding How Light to Go

Luggage-free travel works best on trips using public transportation and making multiple stops. Think of trains around Europe or buses around New Zealand. Other vacations, like cruises, preclude skipping the luggage. Many trips fall in between.

This chapter identifies four factors to consider as you decide when to leave the luggage at home: how you'll get there, how long you'll stay, what you'll be doing, and the physical makeup of your stops.

A. Getting There (and Back)

Transportation affects packing decisions. For example, imagine a week at a resort one day's drive from home. You'd only need to move any extra stuff four times (into and out of the car at each end). That might not be a big deal. Traditional luggage may be the best choice.

Consider, however, driving to the same resort, but from a bit further away: two nights, each way. Now you're facing four additional in-out moves to the car. And the need to unpack/repack (at least partially) four more times at the stopovers. Now the luggage matters more.

Maybe you'll fly or take a train or a bus. That method probably presents at least 12 occasions for moving luggage. From home to the airport/station (2), Around airport/station (1). Around destination airport/station (1). To resort (2). Return trip (6). The total increases if you need public transportation to and from your home departure point or face intermediate connections along the travel route.

On the other hand, maybe someone else -- like a bus or taxi driver or a hotel bellhop -- actually will be doing much of the additional lifting. Of course, more luggage usually raises costs, in basic charges and in tips. And it's rare for able-bodied folks to have help at all stages of a trip, like moving to and from a plane. Then, we're on our own.

Should you take luggage? How often will you have to move it and where?

B. Staying or Leaving?

Staying longer in one place may make taking luggage more attractive in a couple of ways. First, we'll be more likely to see some of the same people over time, so may want more clothes for more different looks. Second, the burden of hauling luggage may be infrequent enough to justify the extra work. The longer we stay in one place, the more the ratio (and hassle) of "travel days" to "total days" goes down.

C. Extra Needs

Sometimes we plan trips around particular activities. Some require equipment: golf clubs, fishing poles, skis ... Others, like a wedding, may need dressier clothes. Combining business and pleasure may require both equipment and dress clothes.

Like everything else in life, the rules change when you include children. Well after strollers & diapers have seen their day, car seats & stuffed animals hang around. And kids' growth rates mean it doesn't make sense to invest in a special "travel wardrobe." However, just as with adults, intentionally picking out lighter-weight clothes and including fewer options (of everything) can cut down on space and weight.

Sometimes you can rent what you'll need. Sometimes you can ship stuff ahead. (We've mailed golf clubs.) Sometimes you can travel in the dress clothes to avoid packing them. But sometimes what we're going to do when we get there means we just need to carry luggage.

Taking additional items, however, makes it more attractive to go <u>otherwise</u> free from luggage.

Compare the difference between carrying a set of golf clubs plus a suitcase and carrying the clubs plus a light shoulder bag.

D. The Layout

When we pack, we also consider how much we know about the facilities at any destination. In particular, we focus on how many stairs (or steep hills) are likely to appear between the arrival point and

the room. The more there are, the greater the advantage of avoiding luggage.

Sometimes convenient laundry facilities mean it makes sense to carry enough clothes to forgo nightly laundry. However, location of those facilities matters. In the unit? Great. In the building? OK. In a resort complex? Maybe, if nearby. Somewhere in town? Not so helpful.

The less convenient the laundry arrangements, the more attractive regular, in-sink, laundry seems.

Spending a few minutes before bed might sound better than a vacation afternoon in a laundromat. Recall that even when machine washing most items on cruises, we cut down on packing by hand-washing underwear and socks.

Once we decide to depart from a "no luggage" approach, the question becomes: how far? Beware. Carrying <u>some</u> luggage, doesn't have to mean taking <u>as much</u> luggage as before.

Chapter 7

You Can Do It

Once you give luggage-free travel a try, you'll never look at packing the same way. Initially, stretching your comfort zone adds a sense of adventure, of getting away with something new. Even after many trips, the different wardrobe and the change from the home routine add zest to travel. You'll find yourself applying luggage-free principles when you do take luggage. Large bags will stay at home.

There is a risk: you may start feeling smug watching other travelers facing burdens you no longer experience.

We toast your freedom from luggage.

Appendix I

How We Got Here

We're retired folks -- a teacher and an occupational therapist -- who have thoroughly enjoyed traveling with no or minimal luggage. The success of our first edition prompted us to rework the topic to reflect things we've learned as we've gained more experience. Here we share ideas that didn't work as well for us, but still might work for you. Or might save you from making similar mistakes. Recall that we receive no benefit from any company whose product we praise.

Our adventure started with a podcast. Anticipating retirement, we started thinking seriously about our long-delayed dream of touring New Zealand. While creating a list of possible places to visit and options for getting around, we stumbled upon the Rick Steves podcast that revolutionized our travel lives. Rick interviewed a guy who had traveled around the world without any luggage. Indeed, without even the daypack or shoulder bag we now take.

The ambitious traveler had used a jacket designed by ScotteVest, which pioneered a wide range of remarkably creative products. Some jackets feature clear windows, for direct access to electronics. Some have removable sleeves. However, their key feature is <u>lots</u> of pockets. Different sizes for different uses, from sunglasses to tablets to swimsuits. Having so many pockets means trying out different combinations to see what works best. A zippered plastic bag with meds in one place, an extra sock on each side ...

The jacket's principal advantage: you needn't carry anything <u>else</u>. Men in particular are not used to having something else -- like a purse -- to keep track of. There's security in having everything in something as natural as a jacket. Roger was sold on the whole concept and used a ScotteVest jacket all around New Zealand. Here he's packed and getting on a train for a practice run:

Similarly loaded, with bumps in different places, Kyanne felt like a mix of the Pillsbury Doughboy and the Michelin Tireman. While she fully embraced the approach of designing a wardrobe for light travel, she needed a different vehicle.

Her solution: the 2.2 oz Sea-to-Summit sling bag we now carry for temporary needs like lunches or souvenirs. Saving the weight and bulk of internal dividers, it has a single storage area. Organizing contents in zippered plastic bags with labels or color codes makes items easier to locate. Squeezing out the air saves space and keeps clothes for collapsing into a bundle. Beware of bags sold for shopping. They tend to be too large (and thus too tempting to fill).

By the time budgets and time allowed us to consider an extensive European trip, we had taken several more cruises and a variety of shorter trips around the U.S., Canada, and Mexico. Those experiences led us to shift our approaches to carrying things.

For Roger, that travel had highlighted some drawbacks to using a single jacket full of pockets. Each time you get to a new lodging, you need to decide how much to "unpack" and how much to carry along as you explore. With the toothpaste in one pocket and the second T-shirt in another, that can actually be a challenge, especially if you're still trying to remember what goes where. If the weather warms during the day (or while traveling), it's less convenient to take off and carry a multi layered (or loaded) jacket than a shell. Although he enjoyed the [smug?] feeling of wearing just a jacket when checking into an international flight, he decided that the daily drawbacks outweighed the advantages. He shifted to the light daypack described above.

Kyanne's slingbag posed different challenges. The narrow, unpadded strap cut into her shoulder. (Indeed, our first New Zealand hostess had fashioned a pad that helped, but slid around.) Further, she tired of the hassle of folding each clothing item into its own plastic bag. Her current daypack has both a padded shoulder strap and enough stiffness on one side to keep rolled clothes from bunching together.

Aside from working through pants options, Roger's clothing choices have remained a steady mix of Ex-Officio button-front long-sleeve shirts and a variety of light T's. He really liked having convertible pants in New Zealand, but Kyanne tired of their inability to allow him to look even a little dressy. The further experience of being pick-pocketed in Athens led him to Clothing Arts pants with zippered pockets inside zippered pockets. They can be inconvenient and their side seam zippers don't hang flat, but they do pass for casual slacks. He wears them when we anticipate crowded cities or colder temperatures. A similar, less-zippered Ex-Officio pair works for safer, warmer places. The convertibles come along when shorts will be handy.

Roger continues to search for the ideal shoes. Beige sneakers worked well in general, but were a stretch in some settings. Sketcher slip-ons added just enough style to fit both casual slacks and shorts. But their lack of laces meant his toes suffered on downhill slopes.

Kyanne has tweaked her clothing choices. She took both shorts and a swimsuit to New Zealand. She wore the shorts several times when it was hot, but only wore the swimsuit once. On later trips, she left the shorts at home and has taken a short, lightweight skirt or dress. They handle the hot days and yet make her feel more comfortable in cities, less like a tourist. She had two t-shirts, but only one woven shirt in New Zealand. One of the t-shirts was a lightweight cotton knit that did dry overnight, but couldn't hold up to the every-other-day wear and wringing out. It lost its shape, and she finally discarded it during the last week. Now, she sticks to synthetic "performance" tees from sporting goods stores or catalogs. She also leaves the swimsuit at home, but has added a second silky woven blouse and has enjoyed the expanded combinations.

Since finding Naot brand shoes, Kyanne is happy with her walking shoe choices. They make flats and sandals that provide enough built-in arch support to eliminate the need for her orthotics. Her black leather flats allow her to walk comfortably all day and are still acceptable when worn with either slacks or a dress. The sandals pack flat and have cork soles with thin leather straps. For cruises, she takes both. The flats are for walking days, and the sandals go from beach to formal wear.

Appendix II

Supply Sources

We list below a variety of sources we have used for our travel needs. Of course, other outlets – both general clothiers and specialty places – may carry items that work for you. We don't receive any incentive or compensation from any of these companies.

Eddie Bauer - We especially like the shell jackets that pack small, their t-shirts and women's slacks, and Travelon packing squares.

Brooks – We like their quick dry T-shirts.

Columbia - Their convertible pants are light, with some inside pockets, and hold up well. Many of their women's shirts dry quickly and stay wrinkle-free.

Ex-Officio – Their men's underwear resists odor, holds up under daily washing, and always dries by morning. Kyanne finds their women's underwear uncomfortable. Their multi-pocketed men's slacks are a bit dressier than convertibles. Long-sleeve t-shirts are especially comfortable.

The men's button-front, long-sleeve check shirts are amazing at staying winkle-free. (Surprisingly, the plaid ones don't work as well.) Many of their women's shirts dry quickly and stay wrinkle-free.

Fox River - We like their socks for their cushion and relative ability to dry quickly.

Icebreaker - We like their merino wool long underwear.

Naot - We especially like their flat shoes and sandals.

North Face - We like their women's pants for the inside pockets and ability to stay wrinkle-free.

REI - We especially like REI-brand men's short-sleeved T-shirts for comfort and quick-dry features.

Rick Steves' Travel Store – We especially like the small, zippered wallet and both the Civita day pack and shoulder bag.

ScotteVest - Travel wear with particular attention to providing extra pockets.

Sea to Summit - We especially like their nylon shoulder bag and similar backpack. Light, simple, collapse to near-nothing.

Smart Wool - We like their socks for cushion and relative ability to dry.

Tilley - We especially like their hats for the ability to maintain shape.

UnderArmor – Their coldgear T-shirt works well alone and is especially good as insulation under something else.

Finally, consider sharing your luggage-free (or freer) travel experience by filing a quick Amazon review identifying the ideas from this book that you found valuable. Learning that you have found success will inspire others to take the leap.

The blank pages that follow are for your notes.

Made in the USA
Middletown, DE
13 June 2019